HOW TO DRAW
PREHISTORIC ™
AND ICE AGE ANIMALS

Mark Bergin

BOOK HOUSE

SALARIYA

Published in Great Britain in MMXII by
Book House, an imprint of
The Salariya Book Company Ltd
25 Marlborough Place, Brighton BN1 1UB

1 3 5 7 9 8 6 4 2

Please visit our website at **www.book-house.co.uk**
or go to **www.salariya.com** for **free** electronic versions of:
You Wouldn't Want to be an Egyptian Mummy!
You Wouldn't Want to be a Roman Gladiator!
You Wouldn't Want to be a Polar Explorer!
You Wouldn't Want to sail on a 19th-Century
 Whaling Ship!

Author: Mark Bergin was born in Hastings in 1961.
He studied at Eastbourne College of Art and has
specialised in historical reconstructions as well as
aviation and maritime subjects since 1983. He lives
in Bexhill-on-Sea with his wife and three children.

Editor: Rob Walker

PB ISBN: 978-1-908177-16-2

A CIP catalogue record for this
book is available from the
British Library.

Printed and bound in China.
Printed on paper from
sustainable sources.

**WARNING: Fixatives should be
used only under adult supervision.**

Visit our websites to read interactive
free web books, stay up to date with
new releases, catch up with us on
the Book House Blog, view our
electronic catalogue and more!

www.book-house.co.uk
Information books
and graphic novels

www.scribblersbooks.com
Books for babies, toddlers and
pre-school children.

Follow us on Facebook and
Twitter by visiting
www.salariya.com

PAPER FROM
SUSTAINABLE
FORESTS

Contents

Making a start

Learning to draw is about looking and seeing. Keep practising and get to know your subject. Use a sketchbook to make quick drawings. Start by doodling, and experiment with shapes and patterns. There are many ways to draw; this book shows only some methods. Visit art galleries, look at artists' drawings, see how friends draw, but above all, find your own way.

Drawing materials

Try using different types of drawing paper and materials. Experiment with charcoal, wax crayons and pastels. All pens, from felt-tips to ballpoints, will make interesting marks — you could also try drawing with pen and ink on wet paper.

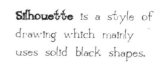

Silhouette is a style of drawing which mainly uses solid black shapes.

Hard **pencils** are greyer and soft pencils are blacker. Hard pencils are graded from 6H (the hardest) through 5H, 4H, 3H and 2H to H. Soft pencils are graded from B, 2B, 3B, 4B and 5B up to 6B (the softest).

Felt-tip

Felt—tips come in a range of line widths. The wider pens are good for filling in large areas of flat tone.

Lines drawn in **ink** cannot be erased, so keep your ink drawings sketchy and less rigid. Don't worry about mistakes as these lines can be lost in the drawing as it develops.

Ink

Perspective

If you look at any object from different viewpoints, you will see that the part that is closest to you looks larger, and the part furthest away from you looks smaller. Drawing in perspective is a way of creating a feeling of depth — of showing three dimensions on a flat surface.

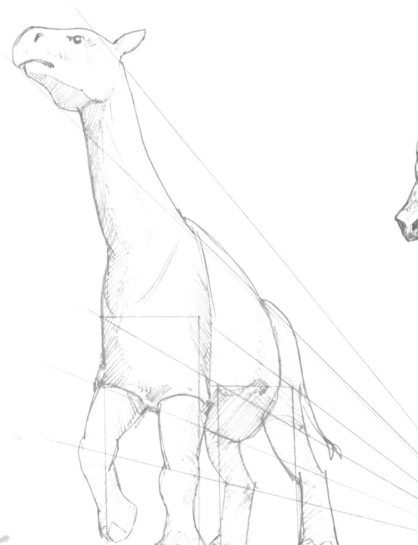

The vanishing point (V.P.) is the place in a perspective drawing where parallel lines appear to meet. The position of the vanishing point depends on the viewer's eye level. Sometimes a low viewpoint can give your drawing added drama.

V.P.

8

Two-point perspective uses
two vanishing points: one
for lines running along the
length of the subject, and
one on the opposite side
for lines running across the
width of the subject.

Low eye level
(view from below)

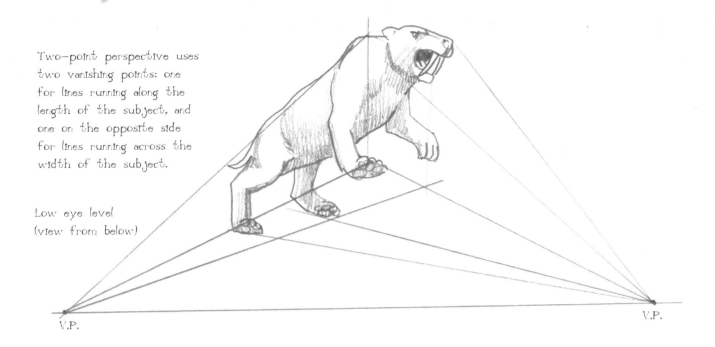

V.P.

V.P.

Normal eye level

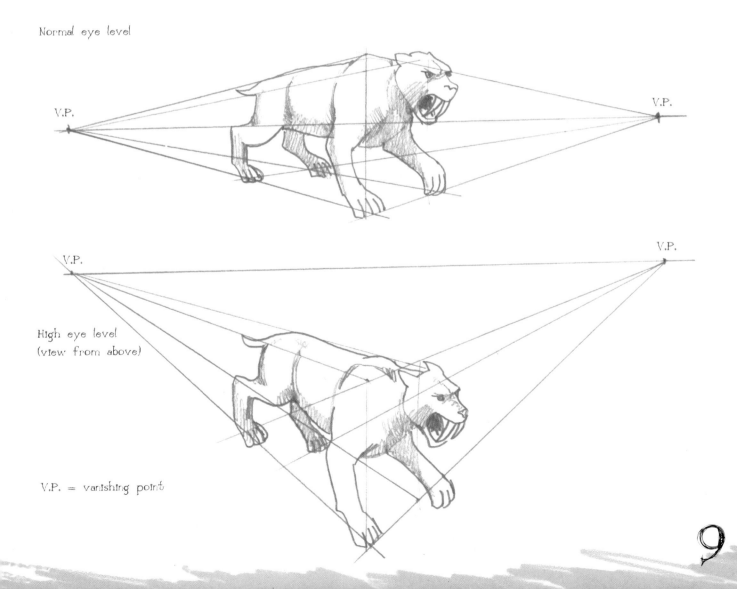

V.P.

V.P.

V.P.

V.P.

High eye level
(view from above)

V.P. = vanishing point

9

Sketching

You can't always rely on your memory, so you have to look around and find real—life things you want to draw. Using a sketchbook is one of the best ways to build up drawing skills. Learn to observe objects: see how they move, how they are made and how they work. What you draw should be what you have seen. Since the 13th century, artists have used sketchbooks to record their ideas and drawings.

Sketching from toys or models can help you understand the three—dimensional aspects of animals.

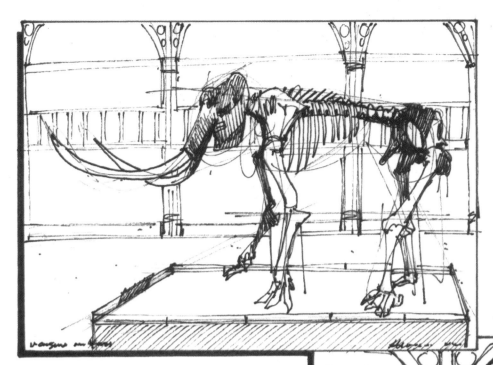

Visiting a museum with
a prehistoric exhibit
is a good place to start
your sketches. It will
help you to understand
the form of the animals
and their proportions.

Try doing quick sketches as well as
more detailed ones — both will help
you improve your drawing skills.

11

Macrauchenia

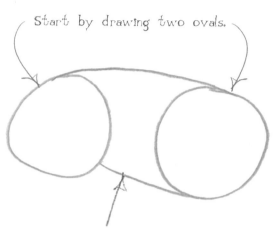

This weird—looking herd creature is found in fossils from South America and lived about 7 million to 20,000 years ago. Charles Darwin found the first fossil of this animal on his voyage aboard the *Beagle*.

Start by drawing two ovals.

Add two curved lines to connect the ovals.

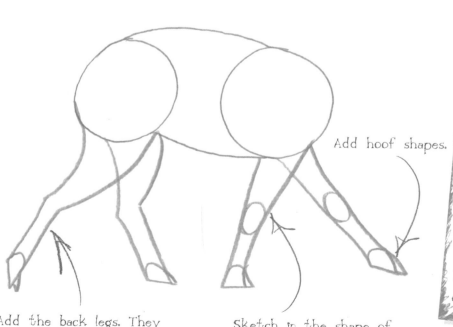

Add the back legs. They have curved lines at the top, switching to straight lines for the lower half.

Add hoof shapes.

Sketch in the shape of the front legs, adding a circle at the joints.

Key characteristics

Paying particular attention to the key characteristics can help your drawing work. Specific shapes such as the head and hooves / feet can define an animal.

12

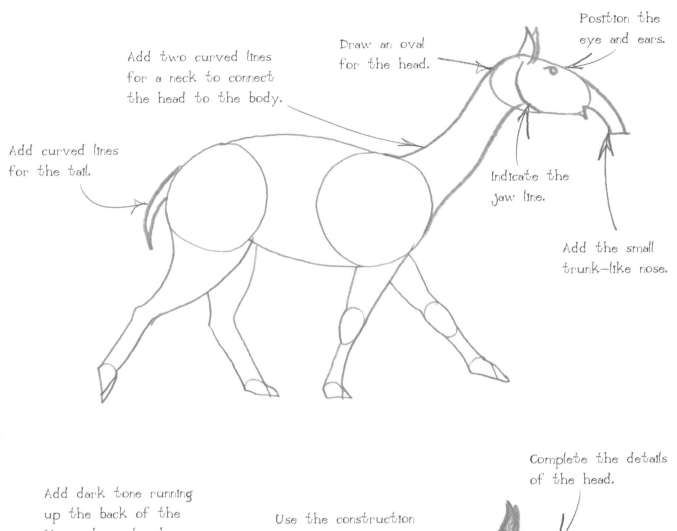

Draw an oval
for the head.

Position the
eye and ears.

Add two curved lines
for a neck to connect
the head to the body.

Indicate the
jaw line.

Add curved lines
for the tail.

Add the small
trunk–like nose.

Complete the details
of the head.

Add dark tone running
up the back of the
Macrauchenia to show
its markings.

Use the construction
lines as a guide to add
muscle structure.

Add a mountainous
background with
trees and grass.

Add darker tone to
areas where light
would not reach.

Soften some of the lines
to create a fur texture.

Remove any unwanted
construction lines.

13

Andrewsarchus

The Andrewsarchus was perhaps the largest carnivorous mammal ever to live. It stood around 1.8 metres tall and was about 5.2 metres long.

Draw a curved line for the spine.

Start by sketching in two ovals of different sizes for the front and rear haunches.

Construction lines

Construction lines should always be drawn lightly. That way you can easily erase them when you finish the drawing.

Draw in construction lines to position the head.

Add simple shapes for the front legs. One leg should bend.

Add the back legs. Use curved lines for the upper part.

14

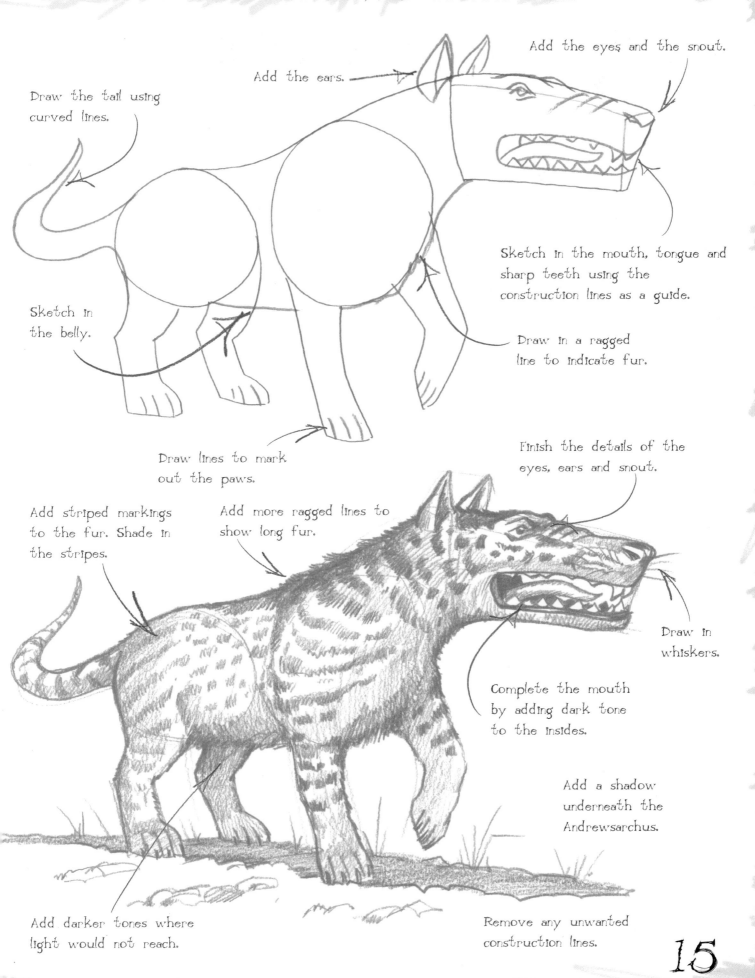

Add the eyes and the snout.

Add the ears.

Draw the tail using curved lines.

Sketch in the mouth, tongue and sharp teeth using the construction lines as a guide.

Sketch in the belly.

Draw in a ragged line to indicate fur.

Draw lines to mark out the paws.

Finish the details of the eyes, ears and snout.

Add striped markings to the fur. Shade in the stripes.

Add more ragged lines to show long fur.

Draw in whiskers.

Complete the mouth by adding dark tone to the insides.

Add a shadow underneath the Andrewsarchus.

Add darker tones where light would not reach.

Remove any unwanted construction lines.

15

Basilosaurus

The Basilosaurus was a gigantic carnivorous whale–like creature. Fossils of this giant creature, measuring 18 metres in length, have been found in Louisiana, Egypt and the Sahara desert.

Add an oval for the head.

Start by drawing a large bean shape for the body.

Add curved, triangular tail fins.

Draw in the tail using long, curved lines.

Add the eyes.

Sketch in the jagged sharp teeth.

Add small fins to the body.

Add two large flippers.

Using a mirror
Try looking at your drawing in a mirror. Seeing it in reverse can help you spot mistakes.

Add tone to the back. Keep your pencil line in the same direction to create the skin effects.

Finish the detail of the head.

Leave white areas along the bodies to show the sheen of the skin.

Remove any unwanted construction lines.

Add some prey for the Basilosaurus.

17

Indricotherium

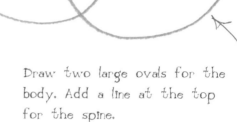

Indricotherium lived around 30 to 25 million years ago. This large land mammal would have eaten the tallest parts of trees in the same way as a giraffe.

Draw two large ovals for the body. Add a line at the top for the spine.

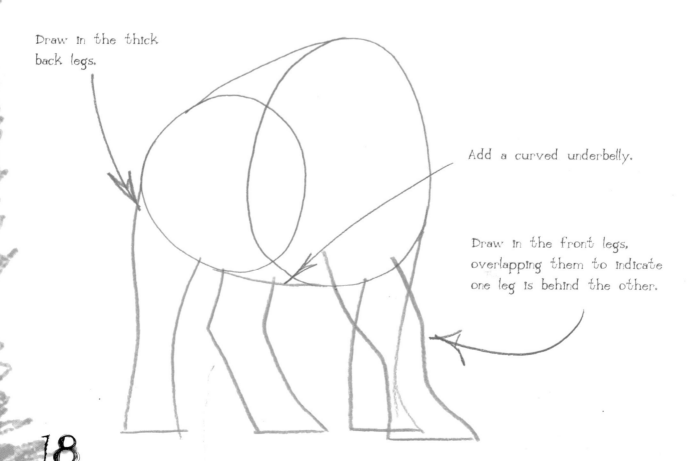

Draw in the thick back legs.

Add a curved underbelly.

Draw in the front legs, overlapping them to indicate one leg is behind the other.

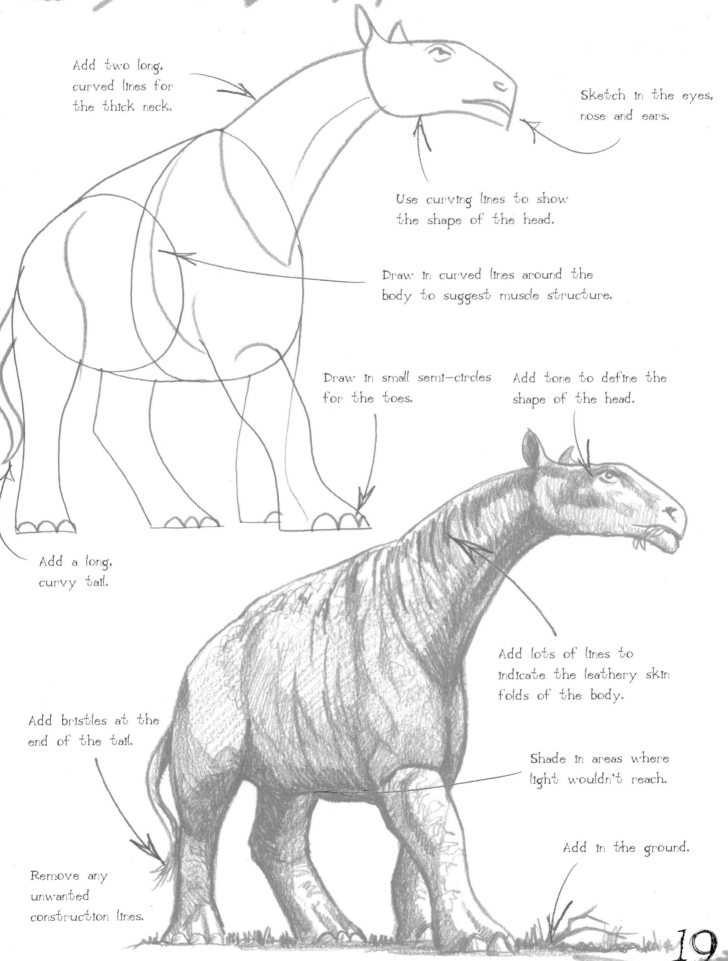

Add two long,
curved lines for
the thick neck.

Sketch in the eyes,
nose and ears.

Use curving lines to show
the shape of the head.

Draw in curved lines around the
body to suggest muscle structure.

Draw in small semi-circles
for the toes.

Add tone to define the
shape of the head.

Add a long,
curvy tail.

Add lots of lines to
indicate the leathery skin
folds of the body.

Add bristles at the
end of the tail.

Shade in areas where
light wouldn't reach.

Add in the ground.

Remove any
unwanted
construction lines.

19

Phorusrhacos

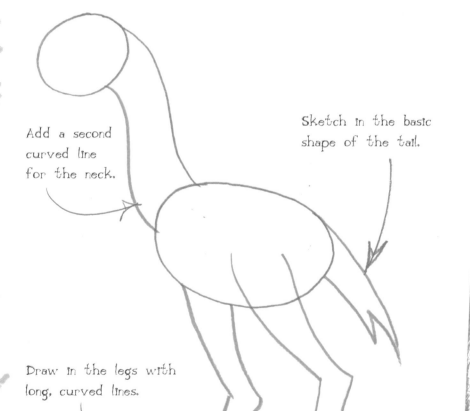

Phorusrhacos is known as one of the 'terror birds'. It stood 3 metres tall and fed on small mammals and carcasses.

Draw an oval for the head.

Draw a curved line for the neck.

Draw a larger oval for the body.

Add a second curved line for the neck.

Sketch in the basic shape of the tail.

Draw in the legs with long, curved lines.

Add construction lines to position the base of the feet.

Composition

By framing your drawing with a square or a rectangle you can make it look completely different.

Sketch in the shape of the curving beak and position the eye.

Sketch in construction lines for the head plumage.

Using the construction lines as a guide, draw in the feather shapes of the head plumage.

Add another line to the neck.

Add a jagged line for where the feathers overlap the leg.

Add lots of curved lines for the feathered plumage.

Add tone to the beak and finish the head details.

Shade areas where light wouldn't reach.

Add toes and talons to the feet.

Add lines to create skin texture.

Sketch tonal stripes onto the legs.

Add the ground.

Remove any unwanted construction lines.

21

Woolly Rhino

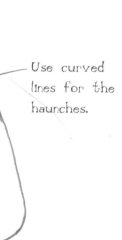

Drawings of these beasts exist in cave paintings made by hunters in the last ice age. They were around 2 metres tall and 3.8 metres in length.

Sketch in the basic shape of the head.

Draw two large ovals for the body.

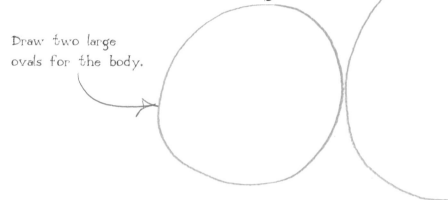

Draw in a curved line for the animal's backbone.

Join the body to the head with a curved line.

Use curved lines for the haunches.

Add the front legs.

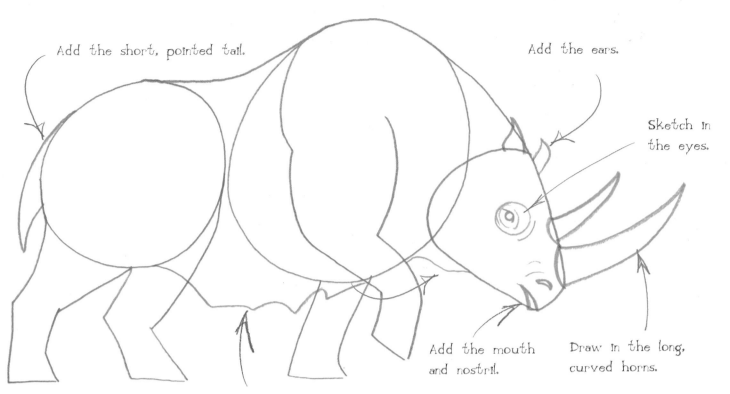

Add the short, pointed tail.

Add the ears.

Sketch in the eyes.

Add the mouth and nostril.

Draw in the long, curved horns.

Draw a jagged shape to indicate the woolly underbelly.

Draw the woolly coat using lots of short lines. Make the lines denser where you want to show shade and tone.

Add dense fur lines along the spine.

Complete the head details. Note how the fur direction changes. Add dark areas to the eye, mouth and nostril.

Add shading to the underside of the horns.

Sketch in coarse fur on the underbelly.

Add the ground.

Add darker tone to areas light wouldn't reach.

Remove any unwanted construction lines.

23

Megatherium

This giant ground sloth stood 6 metres high and weighed around 3.8 tonnes! It lived 1.9 million to 80,000 years ago.

Chiaroscuro

Add dark shading to parts of your drawing for a dramatic effect.

Draw two large ovals for the body.

Add a curved line for the spine.

Sketch in the basic shape of the head.

Add a curved line for the neck.

Draw a long curved line for the belly.

Use curved lines to draw in the legs.

Add long, pointed toes.

24

Add the eye, nostril, ear and downturned mouth.

Sketch a jagged line around the outline to indicate fur.

Sketch in the arms with long, pointed fingers.

Finish drawing the head details.

Draw in the fur using lots of short lines. Vary the frequency for areas of light and dark.

Sketch in a curved tail.

Use many short lines to define the arms.

Add shading to where light won't reach.

Draw in a tree and shrubbery for added effect.

Remove any unwanted construction lines.

25

Smilodon

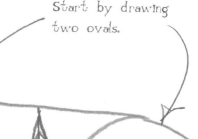

This large sabre-tooth cat hunted grazing animals, pinned them down with its powerful front legs and killed them with its bite. Males could reach 3 metres in height.

Start by drawing two ovals.

Join the two ovals with a curved line for the spine.

Add two curved lines for the neck to join the head to the body.

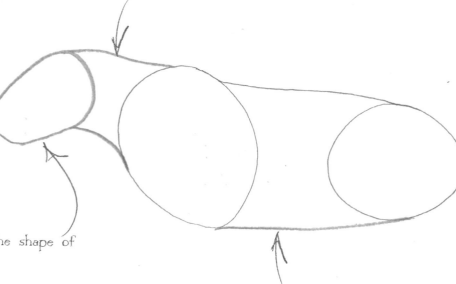

Negative space
Always check the negative space — the area around your drawing. This can help you spot mistakes.

Sketch in the shape of the head.

Add a line for the belly.

Position the
eyes.

Add the ear shapes.

Sketch in the small,
curved tail.

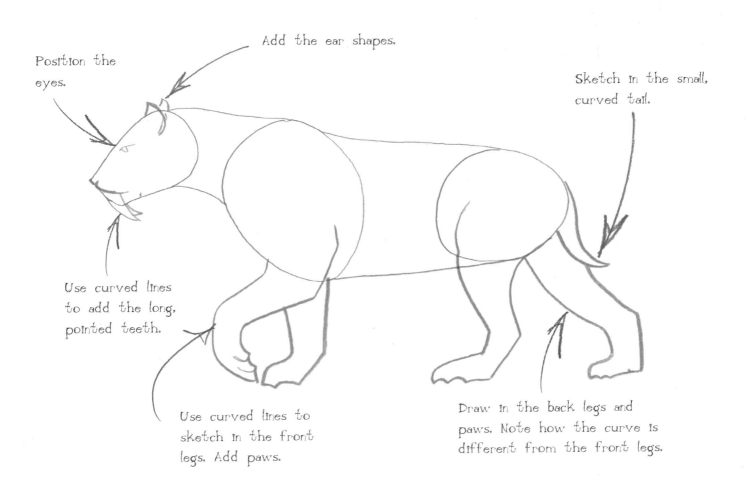

Use curved lines
to add the long,
pointed teeth.

Use curved lines to
sketch in the front
legs. Add paws.

Draw in the back legs and
paws. Note how the curve is
different from the front legs.

Complete the
details of the head.

Add dark tone to create
stripes and spots.

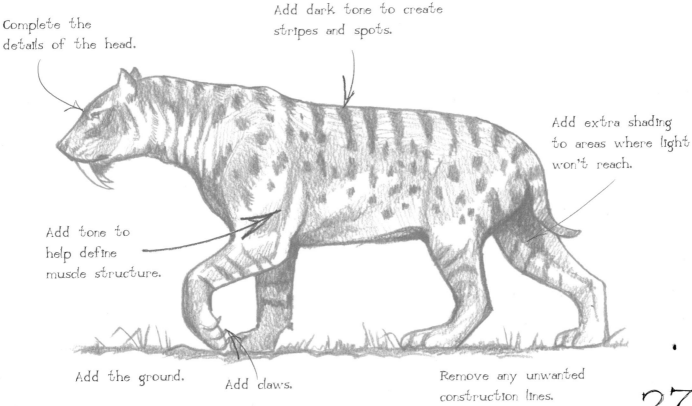

Add extra shading
to areas where light
won't reach.

Add tone to
help define
muscle structure.

Add the ground.

Add claws.

Remove any unwanted
construction lines.

27

Woolly mammoth

These giants of the ice age grazed on vegetation. Males could grow to a height of 3 metres. Bones and frozen carcasses have been found from Ireland to Siberia in Russia and also throughout Europe.

Start by drawing three overlapping ovals.

Add curved lines to link the three ovals together.

Note how the back legs curve differently from the front legs.

Draw in long, curved lines to add the thick front legs.

Sketch in an eye and an ear.

Add a line for the tail.

Sketch long, curved lines for the trunk.

Add long, curved lines for the tusks.

Draw in lots of short lines for the mammoth's fur. Vary the frequency to create areas of light and dark.

Add a dark, coarse patch of hair on top of the mammoth's head.

Darken the areas around the eye and ear.

Vary the fur length and make some areas more coarse and straggly.

Add dark tone to areas where light would not reach.

Add a line of tone to the tusks for a three-dimensional effect.

Add the ground.

Remove any unwanted construction lines.

29

Attack!

A Doedicurus is under attack by a Phorusrhacos. The well-armoured Doedicurus can defend itself with its spiky tail.

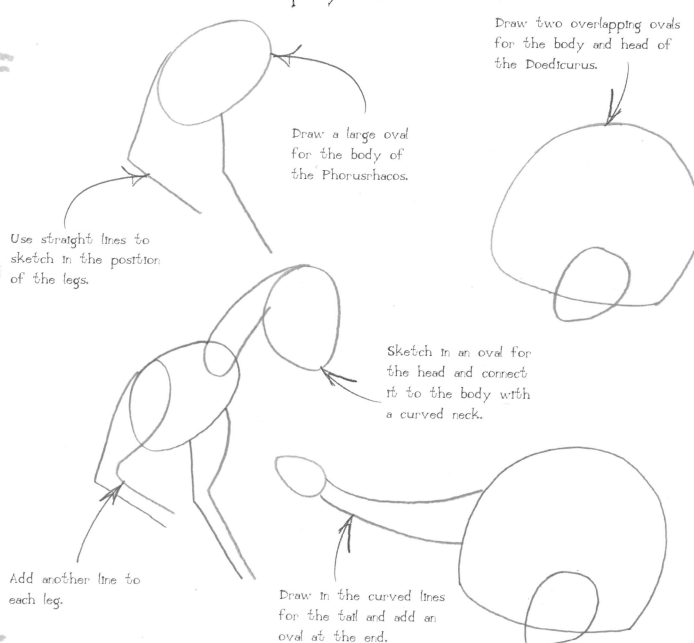

Draw a large oval for the body of the Phorusrhacos.

Use straight lines to sketch in the position of the legs.

Draw two overlapping ovals for the body and head of the Doedicurus.

Sketch in an oval for the head and connect it to the body with a curved neck.

Add another line to each leg.

Draw in the curved lines for the tail and add an oval at the end.

Draw the basic shape for the wings.

Sketch in the head plumage.

Add the eye and beak.

Position the eyes, ears and mouth.

Draw on the tail spikes.

Sketch in the tail shape.

Add armoured bands to the tail.

Draw in the three-toed claws.

Add the legs with three spiked toes.

Add areas of tone to define the body shapes.

Complete the details of the Phorusrhacos.

Draw many small ovals around the body to create the armoured exterior.

Remove any unwanted construction lines.

Draw in a background for added drama.

31

Glossary

Chiaroscuro The practice of drawing high-contrast pictures with a lot of black and white, but not much grey.

Composition The arrangement of the parts of a picture on the drawing paper.

Construction lines Guidelines used in the early stages of a drawing. They are usually erased later.

Fixative A type of resin used to spray over a finished drawing to prevent smudging. **It should only be used by an adult.**

Perspective A method of drawing in which near objects are shown larger than faraway objects to give an impression of depth.

Proportion The correct relationship of scale between each part of the drawing.

Silhouette A drawing that shows only a flat, dark shape, like a shadow.

Vanishing point The place in a perspective drawing where parallel lines appear to meet.

Index